BOLD WORDS FROM BLACK WOMEN

For Noah, Milo, Zen, and Lotus,
and for my mom, Katharyn
and my sister Nefeterius.
—T. P.

To my Jjajas, Adline Mgbakwa Ahanonu,
and Margaret Monica Ntwatwa Walabyeki;
to my mom, Sylvia, and my sister, Adanta;
and to Zena Stewart.
Thank you for inspiring me, teaching me, encouraging me to be myself,
and showing me that as a Black woman, I have a place in this world.
—M. A.

SIMON & SCHUSTER BOOKS FOR YOUNG READERS
An imprint of Simon & Schuster Children's Publishing Division
1230 Avenue of the Americas, New York, New York 10020
Text © 2021 by Tamara Pizzoli
Illustrations © 2021 by Monica Ahanonu
For information about special discounts for bulk purchases, please contact Simon & Schuster Special Sales
at 1-866-506-1949 or business@simonandschuster.com.
The Simon & Schuster Speakers Bureau can bring authors to your live event. For more information or to book an event,
contact the Simon & Schuster Speakers Bureau at 1-866-248-3049 or visit our website at www.simonspeakers.com.
Book design by Chloë Foglia and Monica Ahanonu
The text for this book was set in Moderno.
The illustrations for this book were rendered digitally.
Manufactured in China
1221 SCP
2 4 6 8 10 9 7 5 3
Library of Congress Cataloging-in-Publication Data
Names: Pizzoli, Tamara, compiler. | Ahanonu, Monica, illustrator.
Title: Bold words from Black women : inspiration and truths from 50 extraordinary leaders who helped shape our world / Tamara
Pizzoli [compiler] ; Illustrated by Monica Ahanonu.
Description: First edition. | New York : Simon & Schuster Books for Young Readers, 2021. | Includes bibliographical references. |
Audience: Ages 4–8 | Audience: Grades K–1 | Summary: "This beautifully illustrated book is a collection of quotes from
50 inspirational Black leaders who have shaped the world we live in, from Toni Morrison to Angela Davis,
from Solange Knowles and Beyoncé Knowles-Carter to Meghan Markle"—Provided by publisher.
Identifiers: LCCN 2019052794 (print) | LCCN 2019052795 (eBook) | ISBN 9781534463943 (hardcover) | ISBN 9781534463950 (eBook)
Subjects: LCSH: African-American women—Quotations—Juvenile literature. | Women—Quotations—Juvenile literature.
Classification: LCC PN6081.3 .P59 2020 (print) | LCC PN6081.3 (eBook) | DDC 081.082—dc23
LC record available at https://lccn.loc.gov/2019052794
LC eBook record available at https://lccn.loc.gov/2019052795

BOLD WORDS FROM BLACK WOMEN

INSPIRATION AND TRUTHS FROM 50 EXTRAORDINARY LEADERS WHO HELPED SHAPE OUR WORLD

CURATED BY

DR. TAMARA PIZZOLI

ILLUSTRATED BY

MONICA AHANONU

A DENENE MILLNER BOOK
SIMON & SCHUSTER BOOKS FOR YOUNG READERS
New York London Toronto Sydney New Delhi

CONTENTS

INTRODUCTION

When I was growing up, the wisest and warmest words I heard came mostly from Black women—women like my mother, big sister, and grandmother Lula Mae. They were storytellers, full of tales about trials and triumphs that informed their lives—and mine, too—in unique ways. Those experiences, those affirmations, that beauty and resilience, that love—it's all woven into the fabric of my being.

Their words weren't my only influences. As a teenager, I pored over magazine articles and watched too much television, but I remember that feeling I'd get when I read or heard a Black actress, singer, songwriter, or scholar. My eyes would light up. My ears would perk up. My heart would beat fast as I scanned the pages or listened closely, knowing that these women who looked like me would say something useful and powerful—words I'd tuck away.

Now, as an adult, I still delight in stumbling across words of wisdom from women I find intriguing. Whether I'm reading articles or listening to a podcast or commencement speech, there is a bell that rings in my spirit when I hear their truths delivered in a confident, knowing tone. Perhaps my own background leads me to find these pearls all the more relatable, certainly more precious, when they are delivered by Black women.

It was a few years ago that I had the idea of compiling a collection of quotes celebrating the prose of Black women. There was no agenda other than to bring a great idea to life and create good content. But as I started researching the messages from our most celebrated Black women, this book quickly became a well of wise words I just know will inspire grace, courage, self-love, and strength to take root in the hearts and minds of young readers.

Words do have power. In this book you will read quotes from fifty Black women I find fascinating and inspiring, along with the context of their words. They are writers, politicians, actresses, singers, dancers, scientists, activists, and bosses. From former first lady Michelle Obama to the great poet Maya Angelou to the powerhouse entertainer Beyoncé to the self-made millionaire makeup mogul Supa Cent, the women deliver messages that encourage personal growth and success, a commitment to helping others, and so much more. Their quotes are words to live, love, strive, and thrive by—words I trust will make young readers feel the same way I felt as a little girl when Black women lifted their voices.

The women in the gorgeous illustrations are varied shades of brown, but you should also know that this is a book for *everyone* to experience, grow from, and enjoy. It is my sincere hope, dear reader, that you do.

BOLD WORDS FROM BLACK WOMEN

"There's a **secret** language between **Black** girls destined to move **mountains** and cross **rivers** when the world **sometimes** tells you to belong to the **valleys** that **surround you**. You learn it very **young**, and it has **no words**, but you **hear** it and **see** it all around you. You **sense** it when you **walk into rooms**, your **hair** elevated with every **exalted coil**, your **sway** a little **too swift**, and your **shoulders** a little too **proud**. You feel it like a **rhythm** you **can't shake** if you even dared to **quiet** the **sounds** around you."

Solange Knowles

Singer. Songwriter. Producer. Actress.
(June 24, 1986–)

Solange Knowles wrote this description of the bond that exists among Black girls in a beautiful open letter she penned to actress Amandla Stenberg after the two met. They connected, she said, as "descendants of powerful Queens," ready to sprinkle "Black girl magic in every crevice of the universe."

The world will see you the way you see you and treat you the way you treat yourself.

Beyoncé Knowles-Carter

Singer. Songwriter. Producer. Actress. Designer.
(September 4, 1981–)

Beyoncé often uses her music to say it's okay not to be perfect. Here, she encourages women to be kind to themselves—emotionally, mentally, and spiritually.

"**EVERYTHING I SPOKE, I'VE DONE. AND THAT'S HOW POWERFUL THE TONGUE IS.**"

Missy Elliott

Rapper. Producer. Dancer. Songwriter. Singer.
(July 1, 1971–)

Missy Elliott says that even as a child, she knew she would be a superstar. There's power, she insists, in dreaming big, saying out loud what you want, and going for it.

"It's about getting up when you are down, dusting yourself off, and asking, 'Is that the best you got? Because I have God with me, and I can take whatever comes my way.'"

Serena Williams

Tennis player. Entrepreneur.
(September 26, 1981–)

Serena Williams has always faced challenges head-on as a Black woman in the world of tennis. But the winner of thirty-nine Grand Slam titles (so far!) says here that they've never stopped her from using her biggest voice to stand up for herself.

"**Perfection** is often the enemy of **greatness.** Embrace what makes you **unique,** even if it makes others **uncomfortable.**"

Janelle Monáe

Singer. Songwriter. Producer. Actress. Rapper.
(December 1, 1985–)

This master musical storyteller is often celebrated for being an original and living her life out loud. In this quote from her acceptance speech at the 2012 Black Girls Rock! Awards, she encourages young girls to be themselves, no matter what.

"ENJOY LIFE.

AS IT PASSES BY YOU,

DON'T MISS ANYTHING."

Katherine Johnson

Mathematician. NASA pioneer.

(August 26, 1918–February 24, 2020)

Katherine Johnson delivered these words of encouragement and wisdom during her commencement speech for Hampton University's class of 2017, a year after the world was introduced to her in the popular movie *Hidden Figures*, about how the math genius helped send the first Americans to the moon.

"We learned about honesty and integrity—that the truth matters . . . that you don't take shortcuts or play by your own set of rules . . . and success doesn't count unless you earn it fair and square."

Michelle Obama

Former first lady of the United States. Lawyer. Author.
(January 17, 1964–)

In her 2012 Democratic National Convention speech, the wife of Barack Obama, the first Black president of the United States, celebrates how she and her husband were raised, letting the world know that Black families are American families with big hearts and values that matter.

15

"NO HUMAN BEING

IS ILLEGAL."

Angela Davis

Activist. Scholar. Author.
(January 26, 1944–)

At the 2017 Women's March on Washington, Angela Davis told a crowd of thousands to remember that both America's founders and the enslaved Africans who built the country were immigrants, and it is important for women to remember that history as they fight to protect new immigrants from being stereotyped and attacked.

"To say that in order to be **accepted** we must be stripped of everything that makes us **unique** is faulty in its very premise."

Yara Shahidi

Actress. Activist.
(February 10, 2000–)

The star of TV's *grown-ish* brought the audience of the 2018 GLSEN Respect Awards to its feet when, in accepting the organization's award, she used her empowering words to say that people, no matter their race, gender, sexual orientation, or background, have the right to be exactly who they are instead of playing themselves small to fit in.

"My mother again would say to me you can't eat beauty, it doesn't feed you. . . . What is fundamentally beautiful is compassion for yourself and for those around you. That kind of beauty inflames the heart and enchants the soul."

Lupita Nyong'o

Actress. Activist.

(March 1, 1983–)

Pondering a letter she received from a young girl who felt the actress was lucky to be successful given her dark skin, Lupita Nyong'o shared these words of wisdom, taught to her by her mother, encouraging everyone to remember that the most beautiful thing of all is being kind to yourself and others.

"OPTIMISM IS A MUSCLE THAT GETS STRONGER WITH USE."

Robin Roberts

Television journalist.
(November 23, 1960–)

The *Good Morning America* coanchor and two-time breast cancer survivor told a women's sports summit that it was her positive attitude that helped her get through tough personal and professional moments.

Lizzo

Flautist. Vocalist. Performer.
(April 27, 1988–)

In a 2019 interview with late-night TV show host Trevor Noah, Lizzo says that loving herself and her looks is not a courageous act. Still, she acknowledges that her messages of confidence and body positivity help others love themselves.

"I realize that **my mere existence** is a form of **activism**, especially in the body-positive community."

"Every time we see an opportunity to improve the lives of others, we should **take it**, but that means the people whose lives need to be improved the most **have to have the power** to do so."

Stacey Abrams

Voter rights activist. Politician. Attorney. Author.

(December 9, 1973–)

Here, Stacey Abrams, the architect of a successful campaign to register hundreds of thousands of voters in a United States Senate race that led to the election of Georgia's first African-American senator, is making the argument that the best way to get the disenfranchised the help they need is by making it easier for them to choose leaders they feel represent their interests.

"**Dreams** are the lens through which you **project** **yourself** into the **universe**. And then you have to be **willing** to do the work . . . to make your dreams come **true.**"

Debbie Allen

Actress. Director. Choreographer. Producer.
(January 16, 1950–)

Debbie Allen dropped this gem when a fellow dancer and choreographer asked her in an interview what advice she would give to young performers with big dreams.

"When you've worked as hard and done as much and strived and tried and given and pled and bargained and hoped . . . surrender. When you have done all that you can do, and there's nothing left for you to do, give it up. Give it up to that thing that is greater than yourself, and let it then become a part of the flow."

Oprah Winfrey

Executive. TV host. Actress. Philanthropist. Producer.
(January 29, 1954–)

In her 2011 *Master Class* episode on the concept of surrender, Oprah Winfrey used her deep desire to play the role of Sofia in the film adaptation of Alice Walker's *The Color Purple* to explain how she learned to do her best and then let go and trust that a higher power would get her what she wanted.

"I don't think it is right for kids to grow up thinking that mom does everything. If you see something that you don't like or are offended by on television or any other place, write letters and send them to the right people and you can really make a difference, not just for yourself but for lots of other people."

Meghan Markle

Duchess of Sussex. Philanthropist. Former actress.
(August 4, 1981–)

Meghan Markle wrote this in a letter at age eleven after watching a TV commercial for dishwashing liquid that claimed "women all over America are fighting greasy pots and pans." She sent that letter to Procter & Gamble, the company that owned the soap brand, as well as journalist Linda Ellerbee, attorney Gloria Allred, and then first lady Hillary Clinton. The company later rereleased the ad with the word "women" changed to "people."

"Don't identify yourself with labels and brands and have to buy every cute thing you see. Invest in the things that will grow in equity. That's really the key. Invest in real estate. Invest in stocks. Watch them. Don't turn your financial well-being over to people. Don't lose your house in this mortgage crisis. What can you do? If you have to wash cars, drive a cab, bake pies, do what you need to do to hold on to your property and to recover your life."

Susan L. Taylor

Editor. Journalist. Author. Founder of the National CARES Mentoring Movement.
(January 23, 1946–)

Recalling how poor she was as a young, single mom working at *Essence* magazine, Susan L. Taylor details in this excerpt from an NPR interview how she saved up her lunch money and slept in the living room of a one-bedroom apartment to buy a house in Harlem—and how important a lesson it was to take financial control of her life.

"QUEENS SHOULD ALWAYS HAVE ARMOR."

Ruth E. Carter

Costume designer.
(April 10, 1960–)

This Academy Award winner, who has designed costumes for more than forty films, including the blockbuster *Black Panther*, told the Fashion Institute of Design & Merchandising in Los Angeles that her Wakanda wear was inspired by the traditions and protective nature of women from various African tribes.

> "I'm pretty mutable as a human being, period—if you put me on Pluto, I can figure it out."

Erykah Badu

Artist. Singer. Songwriter. Doula.
(February 26, 1971–)

Erykah Badu, referred to as the "oracle of soul" for her neo soul music and quirky personality, says this in an online magazine interview in response to a question about comfort zones. She goes on to say how important it is for artists to challenge themselves and grow.

Diahann Carroll

Actress. Singer.
(July 17, 1935–October 4, 2019)

When a co-star in the play *No Strings* disinvited this legendary actress to a cast party because of her race, Diahann Carroll threw her own party on the same night, reminding herself that she was responsible for her own happiness.

40

"NO, I DO NOT WEEP AT THE WORLD— I AM TOO BUSY SHARPENING MY OYSTER KNIFE."

Zora Neale Hurston

Author. Anthropologist. Filmmaker.
(January 7, 1891–January 28, 1960)

This respected folklorist, who focused her writings on the struggles and triumphs of Black life in the American South, wrote these words in her memoir, *Dust Tracks on a Road*. She wanted the world to know that even though she faced racism, she was too busy enjoying life to feel bad about being Black.

"**Caring** for myself is not self-indulgence. It is self-preservation, and that is an **act** of political **warfare.**"

Audre Lorde

Poet. Author. Activist. Lecturer. Womanist.
(February 18, 1934–November 17, 1992)

The poet's words are a rallying cry for Black women to practice self-care to keep themselves happy and satisfied, particularly in a society that demands that Black women put everyone else's needs before their own.

"DON'T BE AFRAID TO FEEL AS ANGRY OR AS LOVING AS YOU CAN, BECAUSE WHEN YOU FEEL NOTHING, IT'S JUST DEATH."

Lena Horne

Singer. Dancer. Actress. Activist.
(June 30, 1917–May 9, 2010)

For the longest time, this legendary performer—the first Black woman to be glamorized by a major film studio—sang and danced without emotion, to guard herself against racism. Later in life she realized, as revealed in her quote, how important it is to honor feelings rather than hide them.

Josephine Baker

Dancer. Singer. Activist.
(June 3, 1906–April 12, 1975)

When she retired from performing, Josephine Baker, one of the most celebrated Americans to immigrate to France to escape racism in the United States, adopted twelve children from different countries and called them her "rainbow tribe," hoping to show the beauty of equality. This quote speaks to her hopes for the world.

"Surely the day will come when color means nothing more than skin tone; when religion is seen uniquely as a way to speak one's soul; when birth places have the weight of a throw of the dice and all men are born free; when understanding breeds love and brotherhood."

"Don't you ever dim your light to make someone else feel comfortable! God gave you that light to share with the world. If someone can't take your brightness, politely hand them a pair of fabulous shades and wish them well on their journey. More importantly, pray that they tap into the light God gave them."

Taraji P. Henson

Actress. Mental health advocate.
(September 11, 1970–)

The outspoken actress, a single mom who eventually found her way to the A-list of celebrities after landing her first role at age twenty-seven, shared this thought on Instagram after a morning of meditation.

"You have to persevere. This was my calling. You just have to follow that with integrity and not let anyone take that from you or try to steer you in any other direction."

Chaka Khan

Grammy Award–winning singer.
(March 23, 1953–)

This fiery singer, whose career spans more than five decades, said this about her experience as a star, which, she added, has had as many lows as it's had highs. Still, she said, she's proud that she made singing her life's purpose.

"I just think there's such power in our words, and it's so important at this point in our lives to remember to say 'I love you' to those we care about."

Diana Ross

Singer. Actress.
(March 26, 1944–)

On a morning talk show in 2007, Diana Ross said she named her album *I Love You* because words matter and it's important to tell loved ones how you feel about them while they're alive.

"WHEN PEOPLE SHOW YOU WHO THEY ARE, BELIEVE THEM THE FIRST TIME."

Maya Angelou

Author. Poet. Activist.
(April 4, 1928–May 28, 2014)

In a televised conversation with her longtime friend Oprah Winfrey, this famous poet said paying attention to how people speak about themselves and others is the best measure of their character.

"Be mindful of . . . the way you walk, how you talk, what you drink, what you put in your mouth, who you love, who you bring into your sacred space; how you educate yourself, how you take in information. All of these things are important to understand."

Sonia Sanchez

Writer. Poet. Activist.
(September 9, 1934–)

Poet Sonia Sanchez offers these words to explain that, to her, resisting injustice starts with personal responsibility to one's self—doing what it takes to be healthy, educated, and surrounded, always, by people who mean us well.

Dee Dee Bridgewater

Jazz singer. Producer. Songwriter. UN goodwill ambassador.
(May 27, 1950–)

This renowned jazz singer dropped this pearl of wisdom during a 2015 commencement speech at Berklee College of Music.

"Do not accept the word 'no.' 'No,' when you are going for your dreams, can be one of the most destructive words you have ever heard. When someone tells you 'no,' step around, go to the next door. There is a door that will open."

Alice Walker

Author. Poet. Activist.

(February 9, 1944–)

In this 2004 interview, the award-winning author of the book *The Color Purple* says it's important to pay attention to and learn from people who like themselves and refuse to change who they are to fit in.

"I THINK WE NEED TO LOOK AT PEOPLE WHO HAVE A RADICAL TRUST THAT THE WAY THAT THEY ARE IS REALLY JUST FINE; IN FACT, IT'S PERFECT."

Eartha Kitt

Actress. Activist. Dancer. Singer.
(January 17, 1927–December 25, 2008)

She was one of the most alluring women in the world, but when Eartha Kitt was asked what, in her opinion, is great style, she insisted being happy is more important than having expensive things.

"SIMPLICITY. I DON'T HAVE TO HAVE THE BIGGEST HOUSE OR THE BIGGEST CAR OR THE LONGEST MINK, BUT QUALITY OF LIFE IS REALLY GLAMOROUS."

"Just by deciding to be comfortable in who I am, I am doing something revolutionary and I'm doing something political. My activism exists through the work of my bones against weight in the morning."

Amandla Stenberg

Actress. Activist.
(October 23, 1998–)

In an *Oprah's SuperSoul Conversations* podcast, this young actress, named "one of the most incendiary voices of her generation," insists that being herself, no matter what anyone has to say about it, is the perfect way to fight against stereotypes and attempts to tell Black girls that they are not enough.

"I'm a believer in the power of knowledge and the ferocity of beauty, so from my point of view, your life is already artful—waiting, just waiting, for you to make it art."

Toni Morrison

Author. Professor. Nobel Prize and Pulitzer Prize winner.
(February 18, 1931–August 5, 2019)

In her commencement address to Princeton University's class of 2005, this renowned writer uses these words to encourage the graduates to build and narrate their own life stories, inventing "the language to say who you are" and what your place is in the world.

69

"Self-love is a courageous, radical act. It takes stepping away from blaming others and taking responsibility for our actions and thoughts that got us where we are. We expect others to treat us well but ... how well are we treating ourselves?"

Jada Pinkett Smith

Actress. Singer. Businesswoman. Producer.
(September 18, 1971–)

In an Instagram video about love and self-care, Jada Pinkett Smith encourages her followers to be brave by being kind to themselves.

"NORMAL IS JUST A CYCLE ON THE WASHING MACHINE."

Whoopi Goldberg

Actress. Television host. Emmy, Grammy, Oscar, Tony (EGOT) Award winner.
(November 13, 1955–)

This comedienne and actress, who made her mark in the iconic film *The Color Purple*, created her own one-woman show after being repeatedly turned down for roles based on her unique physical appearance. She also has dyslexia, making her job a little tougher. Still, she's thrived from just being herself and remembering her quote, which she later splashed across T-shirts in her own clothing line.

Jenifer Lewis

Actress. Singer. Activist.
(January 25, 1957–)

A working actress for more than thirty years, Jenifer Lewis recorded her own mental health challenges in a 2018 video, using her experience to encourage others to seek quality mental health care. In sharing her own journey to wellness, she works to change the stigma surrounding mental illness in the Black community.

"Nobody's gonna save you.
Nobody's gonna rescue you.
And nobody can wear your shoes.
You have to make your own bed,
build your own house."

"WHO'S NEXT TO YOU?
WHO'S STRUGGLING?
WHO'S IN THE TRENCHES WITH YOU?
WHO'S JUST AS HUNGRY AS YOU ARE?
THOSE ARE THE PEOPLE
THAT YOU NEED TO BUILD WITH."

Issa Rae

Director. Producer. Writer. Actress.
(January 12, 1985–)

The first Black woman to create and star in her own television series, Issa Rae explains that when she created her projects, she did so with friends who had no track record in the industry, but were passionate about the work. They helped make her projects successful, and they all grew because of it.

"I looked in the mirror and said, 'You're either going to love yourself or hate yourself.'

And I decided to love myself.
That changed a lot of things."

Queen Latifah

Rapper. Actress. Singer. Producer.
(March 18, 1970–)

In a 2013 interview, this entertainer, born Dana Owens, says embracing her body and strong, loving persona helped her focus on themes of self-acceptance, strength, and love in all that she's done, making her career a success story.

"RECLAIMING MY TIME."

Maxine Waters

Congresswoman. Politician.
(August 15, 1938–)

When the Treasury secretary wasted time by not giving a straight answer to the congresswoman's questions during a controversial 2017 inquiry into President Donald Trump's financial dealings with Russia, this California politician repeated this phrase to "reclaim" the right to continue questioning her subject beyond her allotted five minutes.

"If I said to myself 'I'm only going to show up or speak or be visible when I'm perfect,' I would never get out of bed. . . . It's about knowing what I am in this moment is what I need to be. And going for it. The imperfections are actually a gift."

Kerry Washington

Actress. Activist.
(January 31, 1977–)

When asked what it feels like to be considered "perfect," this famous actress says that she has moments of insecurities like anyone else, but she trusts that being herself is what allows her to do her best work.

"Happiness comes from living as you need to, as you want to. As your inner voice tells you to. Happiness comes from being who you actually are instead of who you think you are supposed to be."

Shonda Rhimes

Television and film writer. Author. Producer.
(January 13, 1970–)

In her book *Year of Yes*, this TV executive encourages readers to be clear about what they truly want and living with their choices. The happiest people, she says, aren't just dreaming; they're doing the work to make their dreams come true.

"NEVER BE LIMITED BY OTHER PEOPLE'S LIMITED IMAGINATIONS."

Dr. Mae Jemison

Astronaut. Engineer. Physician.
(October 17, 1956–)

The first Black woman to travel to space spoke these words to a group of students at an annual biomedical conference for minorities, noting that while hearing other people's wisdom is valuable, it is more important to "reevaluate the world for yourself."

Naomi Campbell

Supermodel. Actress. Businesswoman.
(May 22, 1970–)

Perhaps one of the most celebrated African-American women in the fashion industry, Naomi Campbell said this when asked why she still loves fashion and modeling after a decades-long career.

"I LIKE WORDS LIKE 'TRANSFORMATION,' 'REINVENTION,' AND 'CHAMELEON.' BECAUSE ONE WORD I DON'T LIKE IS 'PREDICTABLE.'"

"YOU'VE GOT TO SHOW KINDNESS. HOW CAN I LOVE GOD WITHOUT LOVING YOU?"

Mahalia Jackson

Gospel singer. Civil rights activist.
(October 26, 1911–January 27, 1972)

In an interview on the news show *20/20*, Mahalia Jackson stresses the importance of helping those struggling and those who are invisible and living on the fringes of society.

Ava DuVernay

Producer. Director. Screenwriter. Film distributor.
(August 24, 1972–)

This Oscar-nominated director, who, in directing *A Wrinkle in Time*, became the first African-American woman to make a film that grossed more than $100 million, gave this advice to young filmmakers who want to follow in her footsteps.

"Be passionate and
move forward with gusto
every single hour
of every single day
until you
reach your goal."

"This is for the little brown girls."

Misty Copeland

Ballet dancer.
(September 10, 1982–)

Misty Copeland, the first African-American woman to be promoted to principal dancer for the American Ballet Theatre, wrote in her memoir, *Life in Motion*, that she pushes herself to soar in ballet so that diversity in skin tone and body image can be more accepted in the world of dance.

94

"Don't hate on yourself. Along your journey, many people are going to tell you what you can't do and what you shouldn't do. Don't be that person to yourself."

Raynell "Supa Cent" Steward

Beauty mogul. Motivational speaker.
(February 2, 1988–)

This internet sensation, who built a huge social media following telling jokes and stories on Instagram, had this to say about entrepreneurship after her makeup brand, The Crayon Case, skyrocketed to success, earning more than $1 million in sales in just ninety minutes.

"YOUR ABILITY TO ADAPT TO FAILURE, AND NAVIGATE YOUR WAY OUT OF IT, ABSOLUTELY 100 PERCENT MAKES YOU WHO YOU ARE."

Viola Davis

Actress. Producer. Academy, Emmy, and Tony Award winner.
(August 11, 1965–)

In a 2015 magazine interview, Viola Davis details her family's struggle with poverty when she was a small child. She says therapy, her husband, and motherhood helped her see the positive in her painful past.

"**Dream** with ambition, lead with **conviction**, and **see yourself** in a way that others might not see you, simply because they've never seen it before. And we will applaud you every step of the way."

Kamala Harris

Vice president of the United States of America. Attorney. Prosecutor.
(October 20, 1964–)

Seeking to inspire children of color to pursue positions never before held by people who look like them, Kamala Harris spoke these words as she accepted her vice presidential nomination, the first woman, the first Black woman, and the first woman of Indian heritage to be elected to the second-highest position in American government.